Fifteen Action Steps

Nineteen Psychological Reasons

Ten Financial Reasons

to

OWN YOUR DREAM!

Rent To Own

Crushed By Your Credit Issues?

Get Into Your Dream Home Now!

By Susan Hudson

Own Your Dream
TotalDreamHomes.com
Copyright ©2017 by Susan Hudson

Limits of Liability and Disclaimer of Warranty:
This publication contains the opinions of the author. It is intended to be informational. The author and publisher shall not be liable for your misuse of this material. The author will not have liability or responsibility to anyone with respect to any loss or damage caused or alleged to be caused, directly or indirectly by the information contained in this book.

Publisher: 10-10-10 Publishing, Markham, Ontario Canada.
Printed in the United States of America.

For the most recent information:
24 Hour Information – Buyers (703) 232-1750
24 Hour Information – Sellers (703) 232-1600.

First edition. Third printing.
Own Your Dream
ISBN-13:978-1540321206
ISBN-10:1540321207

Loan Officers
Mortgage Brokers
Real Estate Agents

Do All of Your Applicants Qualify?
Rent To Own Comes to the Rescue!

A gap exists in the real estate market for people that **do have cash** to put down on a home, yet **cannot qualify** to meet all mortgage loan requirements. Our Rent To Own program can get all of your applicants qualified and **returned to you** for a mortgage loan!

Rent To Own is a good solution to solve issues of credit and timing when:

- Existing credit score does not meet loan requirements
- Current credit file status does not meet requirements
- Citizenship issues exist.

Six Steps:

1. Loan Application and Denial

People apply to you for loan approval and are denied.

2. Rent To Own

Ask if they would like to be considered for a Rent To Own program? Tell them to call our 24 hour message line, listen to the information, and leave their contact information for us to call them back.

24 Hour Buyer Message: (703) 232-1750

3. They Move In

We will offer a home we now have, or find them one for our program. Their cash is put down on the home as an "option to buy." It later becomes the down payment.

4. We Get Them Qualified

While they live in the house, we work with them to qualify for your home mortgage loan program. We can raise their credit score by 85+ points every six months. This can take months or years to meet your requirements, depending on the facts.

5. We Keep You Informed

We keep your information in their file and keep you informed. When we start their file and know your loan requirements we will give you an estimate on how long their credit improvement program will require. We keep you informed.

6. Return Them To You

We call you when they meet your credit score loan requirement. We stay in touch to return them to you so we can cash them out on our Rent To Own home.

24 Hour Message Line

Call (703) 232-1750 to hear about our program NOW! We will set up an appointment to meet with you and discuss our program and how it will help your clients!

Immigration Attorneys

Offer More Service to Clients At No Cost to You!

Rent To Own Program

How many of your clients need a home to live in? How many have the dream of American home ownership?

Most people who come to this country have a very hard time finding someone to help them buy a home -- just like they have a hard time finding the right legal professional to help them establish residency and attain citizenship.

You could mention to clients that you offer a specialized **Rent To Own** program tailored just for them. They do need cash as a down payment.

Our Rent To Own Program Will:

1. Help them establish a credit file reporting to the three credit bureaus.

2. Offer them one of our current homes or find them a home.

3. Enable them to live in their dream home NOW as a "pre-owner." They remain in the home and children remain in the same schools.

4. Work to qualify them for a loan while you work to qualify them for US citizenship so they can apply for a home mortgage loan.

5. Speak with them each month about the next action step in establishing American credit.

6. Provide FREE classes to help them pass their citizenship interview and written tests.

24 Hour Message Line

Call (703) 232-1750 to hear about our program NOW!
We will set up an appointment to meet with you and
discuss our program and how it will help your clients!

ABOUT THE AUTHOR

SUSAN HUDSON

Susan Hudson is an independent investor in Virginia real estate. She has previously been a licensed real estate agent in Maryland and Virginia, and had a career as a mortgage broker in Virginia.

In working with clients as a mortgage broker Susan noticed there is a gap in the market for people that do have cash to put down on a home, yet cannot qualify for a bank loan.

There are reasons for this. Successful entrepreneurs may not yet have two full years of tax returns to submit with a loan application. New immigrants to the US may have cash but not have completed five years of US residency to qualify for US citizenship in order to apply for a bank loan.

Rent To Own programs come to the rescue! Susan now helps clients get into their home as a "pre-owner" while they work to qualify for a bank loan. This takes one to five years depending on the issues to be addressed. Meanwhile, families enjoy their homes, do not have to move again, and the children stay in the same schools.

The **Rent To Own** solution may be a solution for you. This book presents Rent To Own :

- As a strategy to solve issues of credit and timing
- Plus nineteen psychological reasons to own a home
- Plus ten financial reasons to own a home
- Plus fifteen action steps.

Dedication To Raymond Aaron

When I attended a Los Angeles meeting in November 2013 I had no idea I would be meeting a person who would offer the knowledge to change my life. Raymond Aaron was a guest speaker addressing the topic of writing your own book. I have been a writer since grade school. Although I have dreamed of writing books, the task seemed daunting. Raymond presented his method and organization techniques to create any non-fiction book, and provides all the follow-up classes and service any first time author needs. Anyone can write a book! A *"gracious thank you!"* to Raymond!

Dedication To Ron Legrand

When I attended a Toronto meeting in April 2016 I met a second person who would offer the knowledge to change my life. Ron Legrand was a guest speaker addressing the topic of earning money through real estate investing. Ron presented his information in a couple of hours and I purchased his program and attended his Quick Start School.

Ron's company, Global Publishing, offers a wealth of education and classes about real estate investing. There are miles of testimonials lining the office hallways. Ron's education, combined with my previous background in real estate and mortgages, has enabled me to write this book. The knowledge I have gained will enable many people to get into homes -- people that may not have been able to do so on their own. I can help them! A *"gracious thank you!"* to Ron!

*A **HOUSE** is made of*

Bricks and Beams

*A **HOME** is made of*

Hopes and Dreams

ACKNOWLEDGEMENTS

TO MY MOTHER

There was always a home office in our house as I grew up. It had a desk, a phone, and an adding machine on the desk. My mother was an entrepreneur who completed the paperwork and accounting for my father's business. She was always the "woman behind the man."

Mother was always a reader. Every night she would be read-ing a book before she went to sleep. I would copy her and read my books written for children. I am still a reader today and in addition to being an entrepreneur myself, my main skill is writing. All writers are readers.

Mother was a wonderful role model. My father was never around. Like many women of today, she did it all as she raised me, her only child. I am grateful! I miss you! A *"loving thank you"* to my mother.

**I have learned
So much from
My mistakes…**

I'M THINKING OF
MAKING A FEW
MORE.

CONTENTS

FOREWORD

I am extremely impressed with how Susan incorporated her research and business experience with her knowledge of credit scores, mortgages and real estate. After reading this book of knowledge that is important to every home buyer I recommend it as a *must read!*

There is extensive knowledge all over the Internet about credit problems, credit scores, and how to handle the issues. Finally there is a book that summarizes the information. This book can be discussed and easily handed out as guidance to help others.

Susan has identified a gap in the real estate market. There are people who do have money as a down payment on a home and may have issues with their credit history and credit score. This book is especially important for people who want to address their issues and raise their credit scores, and for new immigrants who want to qualify and purchase a home of their own.

This book addresses both groups of people. If credit score or credit history is an issue for you then this book is for you too!

You can work to attain your goal for your credit file, and use the Rent To Own program to live in your dream home now!

You too can Own Your Dream!

Raymond Aaron

New York Times Best-Selling Author

Good News!
Rent To Own Programs
Meet A Gap
In the Market!

Do Your Credit Issues Crush Your Dream of Home Ownership?

If you have a cash down payment and you need time to work on your credit issues, then houses offered on Rent to Own programs may be a good choice for you.

- You can get into your home now with your cash put down as an "option to buy" payment

- Then work on the issues that prevent you from being approved for a mortgage loan

- You get to enjoy the house now and your children get to remain in the same schools. You do not have to rent and then move again when your loan is approved.

Rent To Own might be a solution for several types of people. A person who:

- Owns a business and does not have two years of tax returns to submit for loan approval

- Is new in a job, or has a gap in employment

- Has a credit score affected by divorce

- Has a low credit score or issues with debt to income ratio
- Has recently completed military service and does not yet have the next job lined up
- Is a new resident in the US and needs to complete five years of residency to qualify for citizenship

If you are not now approved for a mortgage loan, then work on the required issues to obtain approval. Do not get dis-couraged. Nothing is forever. You have the power of choice in your life.

Your dream of home ownership can start to happen now! You are taking the first step by reading this book! Throughout this book is a set of fifteen action steps you should complete to accomplish your goal of home ownership. Check off each one as you complete it.

Susan Hudson

✓ Take Action!

If you are interested in checking out Rent To Own and Work To Own programs and how our programs can meet your needs, please call:

24 Hour Buyer Information: (703) 232-1750

24 Hour Seller Information: (703) 232-1600

And

Join Our Buyer's List

If you are serious about finding a home on a Rent To Own or Work To Own program, go to our website:

TotalDreamHomes.com

You will be on the list to receive immediate e-mails for houses added to our program. $99 set up fee.

✓ 15 Action Steps to Buy a Home

✓	Item	Action
	1	Pull your free credit reports • FreeCreditScore.com • AnnualCreditReport.com Start a file folder
	2	Compute debt to income ratio • Save your bills and receipts for one month • Create an accounts sheet • Calculate your debt to income ratio.
	3	Make copies of your credit report
	4	Check for errors
	5	List the errors Report the errors to the 3 credit bureaus
	6	Error or identity theft?
	7	**Items 7 – 11 are usually for new US residents only** Look up your bank Contact your bank in the US
	8	Apply for a secured credit card
	9	Open a checking account with a debit card
	10	Contact American Express
	11	Become an authorized user
	12	See a loan officer to complete a loan application
	13	Join our buyers list – Total Dream Homes.com
	14	Do a home inspection
	15	Visit your house several times

I already know
What giving up
Feels like.

I want to see
What happens
If I don't.

1

THINK YOU CAN'T BUY A HOME NOW?

Many people cannot qualify to meet the bank requirements to get a home mortgage loan. There are reasons this might be true:

- You have issues with your credit in the past. Maybe you were laid off on a job and were not able to pay bills on time.

- You have had health issues that were not covered by health insurance. The number one reason to file bankruptcy is huge medical bills not covered by insurance.

- You are a new resident in the United States and you do not have any credit history. Other countries do not do business using credit accounts as we do in the United States.

Do not get discouraged if you do not meet the qualifications for being approved for a mortgage loan right now. Nothing is forever. Many people have handled credit problems, bankruptcy, foreclosure, and repossession and gone on to establish good credit to get a mortgage loan from a bank. Create a plan and stick to it!

Six Step Plan To Apply
For A Home Mortgage Loan

1. Know Your Credit Score

It only takes a few minutes to pull your credit report and get your credit score. Do it once a year. You should know your credit history and score before you apply for a home mortgage loan.

Keep all your credit reports in a file folder so you can see your progress and changes over time. To be approved for a home mortgage loan most lenders require a score of 680 or higher, although it can be different for each lender. The higher your score, the less interest you will pay which means you will have a lower monthly mortgage payment.

Go to:

FreeCreditScore.com

This website will give you a summary of your accounts and one number as a credit score. This is not a full credit report.

AnnualCreditReport.com

This website is owned by the US Government. Passage of the Fair Credit Reporting Act in 1970 came as a result of many needs. Consumers needed to verify what information was in their own credit files. This website is an effort to provide that information for each consumer. This site does not include an actual credit score. Your score comes after you:

- Fill out the form on the website

- Pick the reports you want

- Request and review your reports on line.

You must provide:

- Name

- Address

- Social security number

- Date of birth

 **<u>Action #1!</u>**

Get Started

❑ **Pull Your Free Credit Reports**

FreeCreditScore.com

AnnualCreditReport.com

Or call **(877) 322-8228** and your report will be mailed to you in 15 days.

❑ **File Folder**

Start a file folder of credit reports to see your progress and changes over time.

2. Save Your Cash Down Payment

You need to save your money for a cash down payment. There was a time when you could buy a home for zero money down. Not today.

A down payment of at least 20% puts you in the best position to apply for a loan. Each lender has different criteria to qualify for a loan. A 20% down payment reduces the amount of the loan you are applying for and you do not pay private mortgage insurance (PMI) each month.

If you are a veteran and have military service then contact the Veterans Administration and start your process.

Private Mortgage Insurance (PMI)

An additional charge added to a monthly mortgage payment if down payment is less than 20%. It protects the lender if foreclosure occurs. The additional charge can run up to 1.5% of the original loan amount <u>per year.</u>

---

3. Stay At Your Job

Job history and job stability are important in being approved for a bank loan. Any lender wants to see that you are consis-tently working and earning a salary. Lenders want to see sta-bility in your work and your ability to earn money. Quitting your job or starting a self-employed business makes you look unstable to a lender. If you are a W2 employee you will need to submit two consecutive years of W2s plus current pay stubs as evidence of employment. A loan application will require you to write down your current employment and salary, and it will be verified. Your length of time in this W2 job should be at least one or two years.

4.   Pay Down Debts and Avoid New Debt

Any lender wants to see responsible use of credit on your credit report. Each account on your credit report will show:

- Date the account was opened
- Current balance owed
- High credit limit
- Number of times paid late

If you plan to apply for a mortgage, do not take on new debt with a major purchase. A house and car are the most expen-sive purchases we make. A lender does not want to see you begin a new car payment now. If you must buy a car now, then make 6 to 12 months of payments on the car loan and then apply for your mortgage loan.

Do not co-sign on a loan for someone else, even if the person is your family member. As a co-signer you are responsible to pay the debt, and the debt amount will show up on your credit report.

5.   Get Pre Approved for a Mortgage

Get pre-approved for a mortgage loan when you think you want to take action and buy a home soon. Read the financial section of the newspaper and check the Internet to see the current rates for home loans today.

Decide the purchase price of the homes you want to shop.

Stop and see the loan officer at the place you do your banking. This is simple to do. The loan officer will ask you questions about your current address, job history, and cash in the bank, and will pull your credit report. Go ahead and do this now. This is not a commitment on your part. If you are not approved, then ask the loan officer what items you need to work on. Ask for the copy of your credit report.

Loan officers are on commission for the amount of loans they create for the bank. They want you to be approved and they will give you advice because they want you to return to their bank for your loan. If you are approved, get an approval letter from the bank and submit it with your offer contract on the house you choose to buy. Anyone selling their home will want to see your letter and know you have already taken this step of pre-approval. You will look well prepared.

6. Know What You Can Afford

Know your financial facts and do your homework to prepare for home shopping. Your entire monthly debt payments, including your mortgage/rent payment, should be 36% or less of your gross monthly income (income before taxes and deductions).

How To Assess Your Current Financial Status

For at least one whole month put your bills and receipts in a box. When you have a whole month of bills create a sheet like the table on page 10. You need to know the facts so you can make decisions for the next step and take actions toward your goals.

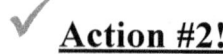
Action #2!

Compute Debt to Income Ratio

❏ **Save Bills and Receipts**

For one whole month put your bills and receipts in a box

❏ **Accounts Summary Sheet**

Create an accounts summary sheet and fill in all the amounts (next page)

❏ **Calculate**

Calculate your debt to income ratio. Multiply your gross income by 36% or .36

	Things to Know About a VA Loan
1	Go to: **Benefits.VA.gov** to file for your certificate of eligibility (COE).
2	Loans are available to military veterans. • Active military members (after 6 months of service). • Reservists, National Guard, and active duty members are usually eligible after 90 days of active duty. • Likely eligible if served on any foreign soil.
3	Does not always require a down payment.
4	The loans are made through private lenders and are guaranteed by the US Government.
5	No minimum credit score requirement. Easier to qualify. Most lenders do look for a 620+ score.
6	Spouse of a military member who dies while on active duty or as a result of a service connected disability may apply.
7	Does not require mortgage insurance for less than 20% down.
8	One time funding fee that varies with amount down and type of veteran. • A first time borrower with zero down would pay a fee of 2.15% of the loan amount. • Reduced to 1.25% with 10% down. • A second time user pays 3.3% of the total loan amount. • No fee for a veteran receiving disability.
9	Show sufficient income to repay the loan.
10	No excessive debt.
11	Use for a primary residence. Not a vacation or investment home.
12	Max loan amount of $417,000 to $625,500 depending on geography.
13	Find a loan officer at a bank who is familiar with VA loans. Not all loan officers have this knowledge.

✓ **Accounts Summary Sheet** **How Much Can You Afford to Pay** **Each Month for a Mortgage?**			
Your Gross Income **(Before Taxes):** Income #1 Income #2 Income #3	 $ $ $		
Total			
Now multiply by 36% or .36 =	$		
	Name of Account	**Monthly Payment Amount**	**Balance Remaining Amount**	**Any payments missed or late?**
1	Current rent/mortgage			
	Installment Accounts:			
2				
3				
4				
	Revolving Accounts:			
5				
6				
7				
8				
9				
10				
	Totals	$	$	
		This total amount of monthly bills should be 36% or less of your gross income above.		

Actions That Hurt Your Credit Score

- Missing any payment on any account, regardless of the amount will hurt your score. It will take 24 months to restore credit with just one late mortgage payment

- Maxing out credit cards. Lowers available repayment capacity

- Shopping for credit excessively

- Opening up numerous accounts in a short period

- Having many revolving accounts

- Borrowing from finance companies

- Lien on file at the courthouse

Actions To Take If You Are Above 36%

If you are above 36% then your debt-to-income ratio is too high to meet most lender guidelines. So you need to reduce debt by paying off some of the bills, or reducing the balances. Do this now before you apply for a mortgage loan.

Make All Payments On Time

This is the first rule of managing your credit accounts. Making payments on time contributes to 35% of your credit score. In the actions suggested below, we are assuming you will make all payments, at least a minimum payment, on time.

If you must take on a second job, or your spouse needs to get a job, then do it. Nothing is forever. A few months or a year of additional income can change your life and your credit score and get you into your new home.

Lenders may not count this additional second income if it cannot be verified for two years. It will help you reduce debt and increase your score when you use the income to pay bills.

Start With Revolving Accounts
Strategy #1

1. Is anything now past due? Make the payment so the account shows current and keep it current.

2. Sort your revolving accounts from highest balance to lowest balance.

3. Make the minimum payment on all accounts, except the account with the lowest balance. On the lowest balance account, make a higher than minimum payment every month until you pay it off. Your goal is to pay it off totally and carry a zero balance. You are not closing the account. Just get to a zero balance and leave it alone. No more charges on this account.

4. When you have paid off the lowest account balance, repeat this for the next lowest account balance. Pay it off. Zero balance.

5. Repeat for the next lowest account balance. Reduce to zero balance.

Strategy #1 will increase your credit score greatly. Yes, this could take months or even years.

Strategy #2

If your revolving credit card amounts are just too high, there is another strategy that will greatly improve your credit score.

Capacity is king and accounts for 30% of credit score. It is acceptable (or not damaging) if you are carrying no more than 30% of the maximum limit on each of your revolving cards. So if your limit on a Visa card is $1000, then a $300 balance carried forward every month after payment would be allowable and still result in a respectable score.

1. On the revolving card with the lowest balance, make the minimum payment, plus additional money, until you get it down to 30% of the max limit. Then do not charge anything more on this card.

2. Repeat until all credit cards are at 30% of the credit limit.

This method will be slower than strategy #1. Strategy #1 lets you take all the monthly payments from the card that now has a zero balance and pay that money on the next card. Since you are not creating cards with a zero balance here, you are still making monthly payments which does require cash that cannot be paid toward other balances.

Strategy #2 will increase your credit score in smaller increments and at a slower pace than Strategy #1.

GREAT
~~Good~~ things come to
Those who wait!
Don't

2

IMPORTANCE OF CREDIT SCORE

Credit scores range between 300 to 850. Your credit score is a number calculation as an assessment of your responsible use of credit.

- Responsible - refers to paying bills on time as agreed
- Use of credit - refers to the types of accounts you have opened and used

Credit Report

A credit report is the summary of all the credit decisions made by an individual for the last ten years. The report summarizes your responsible use of credit. People with high scores have managed credit well. People with lower scores often need assistance in sorting out the information, making corrections and finding credit sources that are a match for their needs.

Your Credit Report Includes:

- All lenders/stores who have issued credit to you in the last ten years
- Whether you paid on time or paid late
- Current balance owed
- Bankruptcy or foreclosures
- Any company that has inquired about your credit in the last 2 years (Example: car payment, or credit card company)
- Court records (judgments, tax liens filed, child support)

The history on your credit report determines what loans you will qualify for and the interest rate you will pay.

- A higher credit score will save you money in lower interest rates. People want to do business with you.
- A lower credit score will cost you money in higher interest rates. Fewer people will want to do business with you.

Lenders are not looking for perfect credit. They do want to loan money and make the interest/profit on your loan. Credit scores are a way of measuring the risk of whether you will repay the money. Your credit score must fit their guidelines.

Credit Score Categories	
Credit Score	**Notes**
300 – 561 Poor	15% of the US population. Difficult to qualify for good interest rates. Lenders may require a co-signer or a large down payment.
562 – 665 Fair	Considered "average" in the US population. Difficult to qualify for good interest rates. Lenders may require a co-signer or a large down payment.
666 – 754 Good	Demonstrates effective management of finances and responsible use of credit. Receive very good or best interest rates.
755 – 850 Great	Top range. Low risk borrower. Receives the best interest rates. Totally responsible in credit decision making and use of their money.

Example:

You want to borrow $250,000 with a 30 year fixed loan to buy a home. Here is a chart to show you how your credit score affects the interest rates you will be charged:

Credit Score Affects Interest Rate			
Credit Score	**% Rate Charged**	**Monthly Payment**	**Total Interest Paid**
760 – 850	3.395%	$1,108	$148,884
700 – 759	3.616%	$1,139	$159,990
680 – 699	3.793%	$1,164	$169,003
660 – 679	4.006%	$1,194	$179,985
640 – 659	4.436	$1,257	$202,601
620 – 639	4.981%	$1,339	$232,095

Scores less than 660 are considered sub-prime loans, mean-ing interest rates are higher because there is more risk to the lender. Work to raise your score and pay less interest. This means your monthly payment will be lower.

Scores less than 620 will likely not qualify for a home mort-gage loan and you need to work to raise the score.

Credit Happy Capitalist

We are a credit society in the US. If you have been turned down for a credit application or loan it is because that company was not a match for your credit score. Their rules for lending money do not meet your needs. Do not worry. Nothing is forever. Credit score is a number that can change every hour and every day. Actions in this book will show you how to create the score you want.

Definitions

Capitalist: A person who has money and property

Credit Happy: The person uses credit to get their money and property

---

Six Reasons Why Credit Score Is Important

1. Credit Score Determines the Cost of Future Purchases

You live your whole life as a consumer or purchaser of goods and services. Many items you will purchase are expensive and you will want to pay for them over a period of time because you do not have all the cash now, or you do not want to <u>use</u> all of your cash now. The most expensive items we usually purchase are a house and a car.

Lenders look at your credit score to determine if they want to lend you money. Do you fit their guidelines? They also determine the amount they will charge you for the time period you need the money. Usually the amount charged is a percentage on the amount you owe.

2. Raising Your Score Takes Time

Failure to pay one account as agreed will show up on your credit report for ten years and reduce the number of your score a few points. A pattern of failing to pay multiple accounts still shows up for ten years and reduces your score many points. This could be 100 points or more. If you do not pay an account and it goes to the collections department you will lose even more points.

3. Difficult to Put A Low Score Behind You

The cure to raise your score is always to change your spend-ing and payment habits. You will need to demonstrate years of responsible use of credit to get that new spending and payment behavior on your credit report.

In ten years the old habits will not be on your report any longer because a credit report only includes the last ten years of your credit history. Your credit score will follow you every-where in the US for your whole financial life.

4. Affects Your Ability to Find a Home

Every person needs shelter, a place to live. Credit score is important whether you rent or own. Even when renting, the landlord will check your credit score because they want to know you will pay the rent and they want to see a record of your financial habits.

Credit score is important in finding the right mortgage loan when you want to buy a home. Lenders want to know your financial habits and that you will pay down the loan every month. A mortgage loan is always the first account listed on your credit report.

5. Affects Your Health and Family

You have peace of mind when your bills are paid on time and you know you have the credit score to buy anything you want. You have stress, and your family may even fight over money, when you have credit issues. Lack of money and pressure to pay bills often take a toll on relationships.

6. May Affect Job Offers

Employers often pull a credit report to use in deciding to make job offers. They interpret your responsible use of credit as being a responsible employee. Are you responsible in making your decisions? Are you deeply in debt and might take bribes to gain more income? All three credit bureaus sell credit reports for the purpose of employment screening. These employment credit reports do not contain an actual credit score number.

How Long Does Information Remain on My Credit Report?

This is the question most asked of the credit bureaus. There are set time frames for how long negative information affects your score. Usually information that is:

- Negative information older than seven years. From date of last activity (DLA) must be removed from your file (Date of last activity means any activity on the account such as payments.)

- Example: You have a cell phone bill that you did not pay and have ignored for two years. If you make a payment today to clear up the bill, today will be the date of last activity. The seven years will start all over again. Your choice.

Federal Trade Commission (FTC)

The Federal Trade Commission governs the three credit reporting bureaus. In 1970 the Fair Credit Reporting Act (FCRA) defined the rules of what the bureaus can and cannot report, as well as how long these items remain in your file.

All information is reported to the credit bureaus by lenders who have extended credit to you. They do not make up the information. They are not responsible for you being declined for a credit application.

The credit bureau simply puts the information into your file, organizes it into a report, and uses their specific calculation to determine your score. Each bureau calculates credit scores slightly differently. This is the reason you have three different scores, one from each of the three bureaus.

Length of Time Showing On Your Credit Report

This is a summary of different credit information and how long it remains on your credit report.

- **Credit Accounts**

  Accounts paid as agreed usually show on your account for up to ten years from date of last activity. Accounts not paid as agreed usually remain in your file for ten years from the date the account became past due.

- **Collection Accounts**

  Collection accounts usually remain on your account for seven years from the date the account first became past due.

- **Public Records**

  Judgments remain on your report from the date first filed. Whether or not you paid them does not affect the time. A tax lien remains in your file for seven years from the date you paid it. Unpaid tax liens remain forever.

- **Bankruptcy**

  Bankruptcy usually remains on your report for seven years from the date filed. (Chapter 7, 11, or 13.)

- **Inquiries**

  Soft inquiries generally remain in your file for one year. A soft inquiry is a company checking you out to pre-qualify your credit for their offer.

  Hard inquiries remain in your file for two years. A

hard inquiry is when you applied for credit to open the account.

Opt out of promotional offerings at any time, free of charge, and you will not receive pre-approved credit card offers in the mail. Contact each bureau to opt out.

- **Consumer Statements**

  If you reported a dispute and it was not resolved you may file a brief statement explaining the situation showing on your credit report, free of charge. You may edit the statement or remove it from your report at any time, free of charge.

**Although no one
Can go back and
Make a <u>brand new</u> start,
Anyone can start from now**
AND

MAKE A

BRAND NEW ENDING.

Carl Bard

3

WHERE DID CREDIT SCORES COME FROM?

Credit reporting has evolved over years due to:

- Mobility of people
- Invention of computers and technology
- Huge amounts of data from an increasing population

Prior to 1960s

Opinions on the responsible use of credit were a local refer-ence from sources in your home town area. Merchants had to make decisions based on their own knowledge and kept lists of people who were not a good credit risk. People read newspapers for notices of arrests, promotions, marriages, and deaths and kept these newspaper clippings in a file folder.

Eventually merchants shared this information with each other. This lessened their own risk and they were able to offer more credit to more people as population grew.

As people gained mobility with modern transportation and roads these methods did not always work well. People began accepting employment in new locations, starting fam-ilies, and buying all the items that families need, including houses. People wanted credit to make purchases and pay for them later. Trust and responsibility needed to be measured. Creating an electronic file, collecting data, and creating credit scores began with the wide spread use of computers beginning in the 1960s.

Credit bureaus came into being out of necessity to track the large amounts of data available about all the people. In the year 2016, credit files include:

- Two billion data items entered into credit records monthly

- One billion credit cards actively used monthly

- This is revolving credit cards only. Home mort-gage loans, car loans, or other installment loans are not included.

Equifax in 1899

Equifax began under the name of Retail Credit Company in 1899. By the 1920s they had multiple office locations in the US. By the 1960s they had credit files on millions of Americans. The information was freely shared or sold to almost anyone. Issues began to arise about accuracy of infor-mation and the right of consumers to know what data was in their file. Retail Credit Company rebranded themselves as Equifax in 1975.

TransUnion in 1969

Union Tank car, a railroad transportation equipment company, acquired some regional and large city credit bureaus in 1968. TransUnion entered the credit reporting industry in 1969 and has grown to 250 offices in 24 countries as of 2016.

1970s

Major technology inventions and the expansion of computer use in the 1970s played an important role in the creation of credit reporting companies. Computers organize, track, and report all the data on an individual based on their social security number. By the end of the 1970s, a few companies emerged as the dominant players. Information scale and availability went from local to national.

Fair Credit Reporting Act in 1970

The passage of the Fair Credit Reporting Act (FCRA) in 1970 set standards for accuracy of credit information and protected consumers by granting access to their own credit information.

- The ability to consistently pay bills on time began to be measured with a score
- Defaults and late payments were recorded
- Consumers can dispute information in their files
- Incorrect information must be corrected within a set time period

- Limits placed on credit bureaus and what information could be shared

- Protection of consumer privacy becomes an issue

- Consumers can now go to the US Government website and check their credit report from each of the three major bureaus:

AnnualCreditReport.com

1980s

Three credit bureaus emerge as the dominant sources to collect, store, and provide information: Equifax, TransUnion, and Experian. Electronic transmission is routine, and provides the same information to each agency. Although these agencies receive the same credit information they use different formulas to calculate a credit score.

Information becomes more accurate as reporting is tracked by the name of the lender or creditor and account numbers. Inquiries are tracked, as well as information in public records (bankruptcy, judgments, liens, child support).

Experian – Newcomer 1980

Founded in England in 1980 as CCN Systems, Experian came to the US in 1996 when they purchased TRW Information. They have grown and are now found in 36 countries.

1990s

Consumers become smarter and shop for best rates and terms for mortgage loans and credit cards. Shopping multiple sources produces multiple credit inquiries in the consumer file. Credit card companies begin offering incentives and bonuses to lure consumers.

The credit scoring models were changed to consider multiple inquiries made within 15 to 30 days of each other as one inquiry. This meant that current credit scores would be up to date and would not be tainted by old inquiry information.

2000 to Now

Massive amounts of electronic information are sent through computer channels, and wireless transmission becomes routine. Identity theft emerges and becomes prevalent because the data can be stolen through wireless transmission and then misused.

Because data can be easily stolen many companies begin selling fraud protection as a service. The regular monitoring of accounts and credit use becomes important for each consumer to protect his or her own credit worthiness and to check accuracy. Selling fraud protection services becomes a stream of income for some companies.

Marketing services to consumers becomes more targeted at identified levels of credit worthiness. For instance, companies with luxury items to sell to high income earners can do a "soft pull" and buy data from the credit bureaus to mail out offers and catalogs.

4

HOW DO I GET MY CREDIT SCORE?

You should print and review your credit report at least once a year. Review it for accuracy. Circle any items that are not accurate.

You have several options to pull your credit report for FREE:

Each of the 3 major credit bureaus will provide a free report of your files in their records. In theory the records should be reporting the same information. You might consider pulling one agency report every four months to always see the latest on your files. Go to:

- Equifax.com   (800) 685-1111
- TransUnion.com   (800) 916-8800
- Experian.com   (888) 397-3742

This US Government website will provide free reports from all three major credit agencies once a year.

AnnualCreditReport.com

The score pulled by a lender for a mortgage loan is called a FICO score. FICO is the Fair Isaac Company. Every credit reporting bureau has their own calculation for calculating a credit score. The FICO method of calculation puts some weight on the mix of credit (mortgage, installment loans, revolving credit.)

- MyFico.com

  Offers a 10 day free trial. You need to cancel within 10 days to avoid charges.

- Equifax.com

  Offers a $15.95 one-time fee for your credit scores from all three credit bureaus. Equifax uses their method of calculation. A mortgage lender may see a slightly different score.

- Make a choice and print your credit report. Make copies to use for notes and for sending in for any disputes.

- Circle items that are inaccurate and need to be disputed.

- Go back to the table in Chapter 1 that lists active accounts. Add any active accounts with a balance to the table if you forgot them.

- Recalculate your percentage of debt against your

gross income. How does it compare to the 36% guideline?

- Are there any items to dispute? Any accounts that are not yours?

- If so, do you consider this fraud? Is anyone trying to misuse your credit? If so, call each credit bureau to put a fraud alert on your account. By doing this, you will receive a call if any new accounts are attempted to be opened in your name.

Errors

Check your credit report at least annually for accuracy. You want to make sure your credit report is accurate and is being reported correctly. Read the list of debts and accounts and make sure they actually are your accounts. If one credit card is used by two people, the other person may have purchased something and that joint account score shows up on your report. This lowers the score when more money is owed on that account. Be sure to close accounts or remove your name on an account if you get a divorce.

Reporting Errors Found

If you find an error, phone all three credit bureaus telling them about the error. You can also report this by mail and include a copy of your credit report. They are required to investigate for free and send you a letter with their facts within 30 days.

Identity Theft and Fraud

Identify theft is a fast growing crime throughout the world.

Anyone with an Internet connection could use your passwords and steal your information. If you see information on your credit report that makes you think this has happened to you, you must call to report it and handle it <u>now</u>.

Call all of the three credit reporting bureaus to make your report. Within 24 hours a fraud alert will be added to your report. If anyone tries to open an account in your name, you will be called to verify this.

✓ <u>Action #3!</u>

❑ **<u>Make Copies</u>**

Make copies of your credit report to use for notes and filing disputes.

✓ <u>Action #4!</u>

❑ **Check for Errors**

Read your list of accounts and check for errors.

✓ <u>Action #5!</u>

❑ **List Errors**

Circle any errors that you will report.

❑ **Report the Errors**

Phone all 3 credit bureaus and report the errors.

✓ <u>Action #6!</u>

❑ **Errors or Identity Theft?**

Is your report showing evidence of identity theft? Or did you make all the charges showing?

5

HOW IS MY SCORE CALCULATED?

Each of the three credit bureaus and FICO has its own method of calculating a credit score and it is secret information. The following information is repeated by multiple sources as being crucial in calculating a credit score.

> **Payment History – 35% of total score**

   Are you making all payments on time as agreed upon?

   • Number of payments made on time
   • Number of late payments
   • More weight on current/recent pay history

> **Amount Owed – 30% of total score**

   How much do you owe for all your credit accounts?

- What is the <u>highest</u> capacity of all your credit <u>added up</u>

Compared to

- Percentage of actual usage

Best ratio is to keep actual usage to 30% or less of the account limits to obtain the highest credit score.

➤ **Length of Credit History – 15% of total score**

How many years has your credit history been open and used?

Within the 15% calculation:

- 40% - current to last 12 months of usage
- 30% - 13 to 24 months usage
- 20% - 25 to 36 months usage
- 10% - 37+ months usage

➤ **New Accounts – 10%**

- How many accounts are new?
- One month old?
- Three months old?
- More than one year?

Opening multiple accounts in a short period of time makes you look like you need money and may be desperate. It reduces your score. When stores offer me a free gift to open an account at their store, I say "no." You should too!

➤ **Credit Mix – 10%**

• **Mortgage**

Always listed first on your credit report.

• **Installment loan**

Installment loans are an exact amount of money paid off in a set period of time. (Example: car, furniture, student loan)

Installment loans help raise your score and are better than revolving credit card accounts.

• **Revolving credit**

Revolving credit is a card with a set limit. You make at least a minimum payment each month and are not required to pay the entire balance at any time. Having too many revolving credit accounts lowers your score (Examples: retail store accounts, gasoline credit cards)

A
YEAR
From now
You will wish you had started
TODAY.

Karen Lamb

6

THREE CREDIT BUREAUS

You will have three credit scores from three different bureaus. Each bureau uses a different formula and combines your information to assign a credit score. Your score can change every day. Mortgage lenders will use your middle score of the three scores as the one score to qualify you for a loan.

Examples: 650 **666** 680

- You might make a payment today which reduces the amount you owe and your score goes up.
- On the same day you might open a new account and buy something which increases your debt. You owe more money and your score goes down.

Your credit score is like a recipe for food.

- You may add more sugar to the brownies which increases the calorie count.

- Then you add nuts to the brownies which also increases the calorie count.

- Then you use low calorie margarine instead of butter to lower the calorie count.

Every hour or every day your credit score might change depending on your use of your credit, payments made, and charges added.

3 Credit Bureaus in the US		
Equifax	Equifax.com Box 740241 Atlanta GA 30374	800 685 1111 Credit report inquiries 866 238 6559 Disputes 888 766 0008 Fraud Alert
TransUnion	TransUnion.com Box 2000 Chester PA 19022 Dispute.transunion.com	800 888 4213 Get free annual report 800 916 8800 Disputes
Experian	Experian.com Box 4500 Allen TX 75013	888 397 3742 Credit report 800 509 8495 Disputes

7

ESTABLISHING NEW CREDIT IN THE US

If you are an international student or new resident wanting to become a US citizen you will find o ut q uickly t hat y our credit history from your home country does not follow you to the United States. Attaining credit can be difficult. You are starting from zero.

You need to open credit accounts in your name here in the US. Even if you plan to return to your home country, you will find it difficult to live in the US without a credit card. There are some things that always require a credit card, like renting a car. Landlords and utility companies will check credit history if you apply to rent a home or apartment.

Understand The Importance Of Building Credit

Any American lender will want to check your credit history

with the major US credit bureaus. You must build a strong credit history that can be tracked and verified here in the US. Other countries do not report credit history to our US credit bureaus.

Does the Bank In Your Home Country Have a Branch In the US?

Look up your bank on the Internet and see if there are listings for a US location. Bank of Pakistan, and Bank of Taiwan and many others have locations in Washington, DC. Call the US location in any US city and ask if they will issue an American credit card to you that will report to the three American credit bureaus. (TransUnion, Experian, Equifax)

Create Your New Credit File

Secured credit cards are usually easy to get because you deposit your money in a savings account as collateral in case you don't pay the bill. The credit card company holds your money as a guarantee. This reduces risk and is a good option for people who have credit issues.

Start With A Secured Credit Card

A secured card requires that you deposit money in a savings account to guarantee that you will pay the credit card bill. You need to complete an application and send in the money. Different cards require different amounts.

Once you have opened this secured card do not apply for any other new cards that come in the mail or this will trigger a hard inquiry. A hard inquiry is an application for a new credit account requested by you. It shows on your credit report.

This could be bad if you apply for too many accounts in a short period of time. Looking for credit makes you appear as needing money.

You will need:

- Permanent address
- Social security number (US citizens or permanent resident only) or a federal taxpayer ID number
- A job to earn money
- A bank account to pay bills

Alternatives If You Need Them

- Open a US checking account and get a debit card. This will give you convenience for routine spending. It does not establish credit.

- If you had an American Express card in your home country for over one year, contact the Amex office in your country and ask if they will open an Amex account for you in the US.

- Open an account with an international bank in your home country if it has branches here in the US. That bank may be more willing to extend credit to you here in the US since you are already their customer.

- Once your secured card is established and reporting correctly you can apply for more credit accounts. Slowly. Establish no more than one or two accounts per year. Consider stores such as Target, Sears, and WalMart.

Maximize Your First Card

Be sure your first credit card reports to the three American credit bureaus. Use it regularly for small purchases. Always pay on time.

Become An Authorized User

If you have relatives already here in the US, you might become an authorized user on their existing credit card. Your relative can call the company and add you as an authorized user. You will receive your own card with your name on it. Your relative is the sole owner and is responsible for paying charges on the card.

The purchases and payments will show as good data on your credit report. After being an authorized user for at least six months, go to **AnnualCreditReport.com** and pull your credit report annually for free. Check to see if the data is showing up correctly.

Secured Credit Cards

Here are 3 secured credit cards to consider. Apply for <u>ONE</u> of these as your first credit card. Go online to apply. I am <u>not</u> <u>endorsing</u> these cards. These cards and others come up when you key in "secured credit cards" for an Internet search.

1	**Capital One Secured Master Card** CapitalOne.com Customer Service: (844) 348-8652 • Deposit: $49, $99, or $200 to open your account. • You can pay the deposit over time and increase the deposit amount. • Receive a higher credit line after 5 payments made on time. • Yes, reports to the major credit bureaus. • Annual fee: $0.
2	**US Bank Secured Discover Card** DiscoverCard.com Customer Service: (800) 315-1776 • Deposit: up to $5000 • Yes, reports to major credit bureaus • May be eligible for upgrade in 12 months • Annual fee: $0
3	**Open Sky Secured Visa Credit Card** OpenSkyCC.com (855) 763-6736 • Deposit: $200 to $3000 • No credit check. Almost everyone accepted. • Do not need a bank account • Annual fee: $35

✓ Action #7!

□ **Look Up Your Bank**

Look up your bank on the Internet and check for listings of a US location.

□ **Contact Your Bank in the US**

Will they issue an American credit card to you that will report to all 3 bureaus?

✓ Action #8!

□ **Apply for a Secured Card**

Complete the application and send in money to open the account. Make sure this card reports to the 3 credit bureaus.

✓ Action #9!

□ **Open a Checking Account That Offers a Debit Card**

Visit a local bank to open a checking account that offers a debit card for routine spending.

✓ **<u>Action #10!</u>**

❑ **Contact American Express**

If you had American Express in your home country, contact that office and ask if they will open an account for you in the US.

✓ **Action #11!**

❑ **Become An Authorized User**

Check with a relative or friend already here in the US who will trust you to add you to their existing account.

To Create a Credit Score
You need at least one active credit account that is at least 6 months old and is reporting to the 3 credit bureaus. (Equifax, Trans Union, Experian)

Pass Your Citizenship Test!

Rent To Own pre-owners in our houses are offered **FREE** preparation classes to study for citizenship exams. There are three parts to the exam: (1) your interview, (2) writing English, and (3) correctly answering ten of one hundred possible questions on US history and government.

Classes are three hours long and are usually held on Saturdays in Reston, Virginia. Each class covers one of the three exam parts. You may attend as many as you like until you pass your exam!

8

CREDIT LANGUAGE

While working on your credit and shopping for a home mortgage loan you will come across many terms that need to be defined. These finance terms are a start.

Unsecured Card vs Secured Card

Unsecured credit cards are the most common type of revolv-ing credit card. This month you have a balance, make at least a minimum payment, and you can keep charging. They revolve in that they never end. Of course, you can pay off the balance to zero and leave the account open in case you need it again. They are not secured by any type of collateral or property that the lender can repossess if the payment is not made. The issuer of the card must go to court or garnish wages to recover the money.

Secured credit cards are opened by creating a savings account first. Money is deposited and held in the account as a guarantee in case the bill is not paid. If bills are not paid the issuer of the card will take the savings account and does not go to court or garnish wages.

Secured credit cards are the easiest way to start a credit file for new immigrants in the US. You can add new clean credit to your file if you have had bad credit and accounts closed down in the past. Be sure to choose a card that reports to the three major credit bureaus.

Soft Pull vs Hard Pull

A soft pull is a company with a legitimate business purpose doing research on you to see if you are eligible for their product. It will be listed on your report and is NOT factored into your credit score.

A hard pull is when you actually applied for credit and a company has accessed your credit report to see if you qualify. These hard pulls show up for two years on your report. They are a minor influence, maybe 10% of your rating.

Fixed Rate Mortgage

A fixed rate loan has the same rate for the entire length of the loan. The most common loans in this category are 30 year fixed and 15 year fixed. The monthly payment will never change for the life of the loan. The taxes and insurance may change over time.

Your monthly payment will be principal, interest, taxes, and insurance (PITI). So be sure to add the taxes and insurance to the quoted payment each month to calculate your monthly payment.

Adjustable Rate Mortgage

Adjustable rate mortgages (ARM) have an interest rate that will change or "adjust" on a given schedule. There are no surprises. It is all in writing. The first few years the rate will be lower to allow you to get into the house. In a few years you may be earning more money in your job and can afford to make higher payments as your income rises. Or, perhaps you only plan to be in this house for a few years and do not intend to own this house. You will sell it and move on.

Conventional Loan

A conventional loan is one offered by any lending institution. It is not insured or guaranteed by the federal government in any way. If you do not make the payments and the house goes to foreclosure, the bank will auction the house on the courthouse steps.

US Government Mortgage Sources

- **Veterans Administration (VA)**

   The Veterans Administration offers loan programs at slightly lower interest rates to military veterans as a reward for their service in uniform. These loans are available to any military person with no money down. The loan is guaranteed by the federal government. If the veteran does not make his or her payments the government guarantees to pay the lender for the loan amount.

- **Federal Housing Authority (FHA)**
  The FHA is a mortgage insurance program managed by the Department of Housing and Urban Development (HUD). The government is guaranteeing the lender that they will pay the lender if you do not make the payments. This program allows you to put as little down as 3.5% of the purchase price. You do have to pay private mortgage insurance each month (PMI).

- **Department of Agriculture (USDA)**
  The USDA has a loan program for buyers of rural property who meet certain requirements. They must have a low income and not be able to obtain conventional financing loans.

Jumbo Loan/Non-Conforming Loan

A jumbo loan exceeds the conforming loan limits of Fannie Mae and Freddie Mac. This loan has a higher risk for the lender because of the huge loan size. Borrowers must have excellent credit and larger down payments. Interest rates are usually higher.

Conforming Loan

A conforming loan meets dollar amount guidelines of Fannie Mae or Freddie Mac. These two companies buy loans from lenders who made loans and then sell them to Wall Street investors. A conforming loan falls within Fannie/Freddie guidelines.

Jumbo Loan

In Fairfax County Virginia jumbo/non-conforming loans are $625,000 and above Check your area.

Conforming Loan

In Fairfax County Virginia a conforming loan is any amount below $625,000. Check your area.

9

SHOPPING FOR A
HOME MORTGAGE

The real estate market has been changing over the past few years. Home interest rates are still very low. Home values tend to rise slightly faster than inflation. In 66% of metro areas home buyers can break even in about two years so that the costs of buying a home are recovered by the appreciation gained in the value of the home.

Statistics on the real estate site Zillow show:

- More than half of renters (53%) say financial limitations are an issue and they do not qualify to meet bank requirements for mortgage approval.

- Other renters (20%) just prefer to rent because of issues with their income, savings, or debt. They avoid the commitment.

- Of all renters, about 82% are long term renters in the same home.
- Of all renters, about 14% say they do not stay in the same location long enough to buy.

2008 Crisis in the US

Home prices have mostly recovered their values from the 2008 crisis created by no money down loans, and over lenient qualification requirements. For years prior to 2008 many home buyers chose Adjustable Rate Mortgages (ARM) that started out at a low interest rate that was easily affordable.

When those 1 year, 3 year, 5 year, 7 year, and even 10 year ARM loans converted to their market interest rate the payments became so high that homeowners could no longer make their payments. Many houses went to foreclosure and this was a main cause of the 2008 financial crisis. Because of this history, requirements for home mortgage loan applications have once again become conservative. You need a strong down payment, usually 20%.

In today's market rents are climbing fast and suddenly home ownership is now attractive again. Yet job stability and income amounts have not kept pace. People cannot afford to buy a home or cannot qualify for a loan. Credit scores above 720 are receiving most of the new loans. Lenders are taking longer to process each loan because they verify every detail of the application. This slowdown is not likely to change quickly.

Mortgage Payments

All mortgage payments are due the first of each month. You can actually pay until the 15th of each month and usually there is no late charge. If paid after the 15th of the month, there will be a late charge. You must make the monthly payment by the last day of month or it will show up as late on your credit report. Make the payment on line or send it overnight if needed.

Choose Your Loan Type

Do shop around for a mortgage. Every bank has a loan officer who will give you information about loans offered by that bank. Different banks have different programs and different requirements to qualify for a loan. You need to learn about loan qualifications and choose the type of loan that fits your money and your life.

Learn about loans and choose the best one for you. Choosing the wrong loan with payment requirements that you cannot meet will bring you stress and problems. If you do not make your payments the bank may foreclose and evict you from your house. This will never happen as long as you make your payments as agreed upon on the required date each month. Be sure to choose a house and loan program that fits your budget. Buying a bigger house also means paying bigger utility bills.

Factors That May Differ At Each Bank:

- Interest rate

- Closing costs

- Down payment amount required (often 20%)

- Private mortgage insurance (charged for less than 20% down)

- Pre-payment penalty

Types Of Loans

There are many loans offered by lending institutions. These are the three types of loans offered by most banks. Choose the one that meets your goals.

- **30 Year Fixed**

  Goal: Pay off the loan in 30 years and own your house free and clear. You paid for the house.

  The 30 year fixed loan is a traditional and safe mortgage for buying a home. Even though your loan may be a 30 year loan, you can make extra payments each year if you have the extra money and choose to do so. For instance make 13 payments each year instead of 12 and you will pay off a 30 year loan in 21 years.

- **15 Year Fixed**

  Goal: Pay off the loan in 15 years and own your house free and clear. You paid for the house.

  The 15 year fixed loan is for people who have good income and a stable career now and want to pay off the mortgage to own the house in 15 years. This loan charges a lower interest rate than a 30 year fixed loan. The monthly payment amount is higher because you are paying for the house in 15 years instead of 30 years.

- **Adjustable Rate Mortgage (ARM)**

  Goal: Get into your house now at a lower monthly payment because your interest rate is lower to start. You are sure your income will rise in the future, or you are sure you will be moving in the future.

3 Year ARM Example

- In years 1 – 3 your interest rate may be 2.5%.
- For years 1 to 3 your payments might be $1,000 each month, plus taxes and insurance.
- Then at the start of the fourth year the interest rate will rise to market rate and stay the same to year 30.
- Your payment will be higher at 5% or 6%. Perhaps $1,250 each month to year 30. You will own your home at the end of the mortgage.
- You are sure you will earn more income in the next 1, 3, 5, 7, or 10 years, or
- You will not live in the house longer than 3 years and will sell it. You do not intend to own this house.

Do A Home Inspection

Every house requires repairs and upkeep. When they find the home they want, most people do a home inspection. Home inspections are not required. You are asking a knowledgeable person to inspect the house, plumbing, wiring, roof, and appliances. He or she will write up a report and give it to you in a notebook all about the condition of the house. This report will tell you if something is not working now or will need to be replaced soon.

You want to know this information so you can plan for replacement costs in the future. If you are not happy with the information in the report, usually you can cancel the house purchase. Most people go forward with the purchase and handle the repairs when they are needed.

Some house repairs involve an opinion. One person's opinion is to replace the roof because it is 10 years old. Another person's opinion is not to replace it because a roof can last 20+ years. Some roofs have a 50 year guarantee. You decide whether you want to accept the information in your home inspection report.

The price of a home inspection is based on the purchase price of the house. An expensive house will have a higher fee.

Visit Your House Several Times

When you have chosen the house you want, drive by the house several times at different times of day, on a weekday or weekend, and in different weather. Check out the neighborhood. Even talk to neighbors if they are outside. Ask them:

- How long they have lived there?
- What do they like about the neighborhood?
- Who are the other neighbors?
- Are there any children in the neighborhood?

Rent To Own is a good way to experience the house before you actually own it.

Loan Applications

The actual loan application is always the same. Get one copy from any lending institution and complete it. Then make copies. It requires time and a lot of information you will need to look up. Leave the signature line blank. Each loan application needs an original signature.

✓ ## Action #12!

❑ **Complete a Mortgage Loan Application**

Go to a bank and ask to speak to the loan officer. Discuss loans that apply to you. This is not a commitment. Ask for the loan application to take home and fill out. Or, if he/she insists complete it in front of him/her and ask them to make a copy for you.

✓ ## Action #13!

❑ **Join Our Buyer's List** If you are serious about finding a home on a Rent to Own or Work to Own Program, go to our website **TotalDreamHomes.com** and join our buyers list. You will be on the list to receive immediate e-mails for houses added to our program. $99 set up fee.

✓ ## Action #14!

❑ **Do a Home Inspection**

Do a home inspection on your chosen home for an opinion about the condition of the house and any anticipated repairs.

✓ ## Action #15!

❑ **Visit Your House**

Drive by your house several times on different days and in different weather. Talk to neighbors, meet them, and ask them about the neighborhood.

Doubt kills more dreams

THAN FAILURE EVER WILL.

10

NINETEEN PSYCHOLOGICAL VALUES OF HOME OWNERSHIP

People need shelter. You need a place to live and be protected. The d esire t o o wn a h ome u sually b rings h uge p sychological benefits. Financial benefits will be included in the next chapter.

1. Home Ownership Is a Cornerstone

Home ownership matters to people, communities, and is a cornerstone to American freedom. When early settlers came to America in the 1600s they came from countries that were owned and governed by kings and queens. The king or queen owned everything, and peasants owned nothing. There w ere only two classes of people, nobility and peasants.

Early settlers arriving in America saw unlimited land with trees for wood to build houses, and beautiful rivers for water, irrigation, and transportation. The land was there for the taking. Few royals ever saw America. They only sent emissaries to look it over and bring the stories home.

2. Home Ownership Is Mental

Americans have always enjoyed wide open space. We think wide and open *about* space. We like a formal dining room and a kitchen area eating space. We like a formal living room and a separate family room. We like to build space into our houses because space was unlimited. Even American Indians roamed the plains and enjoyed unlimited space. An original one room log cabin had infinite acreage to build more rooms. Americans like to *own* space and personalize it to our needs.

Home ownership is an American dream with benefits that renting a home does not offer. It is a huge building block that creates a stable environment for individuals, families, and neighborhoods. The possibility to own a home is a foundation for family goals and security. Home ownership is a safe long term investment.

3. Confidence and Pride of Ownership

A home is usually the most expensive item purchased in life. Because they made the effort to save money for a down payment and now actually own a home, people feel confident in their ability to manage their finances and make the right choices. Confidence and pride in attaining this huge goal are a wonderful feeling. You are now more than an individual. You are a member of a community who belongs, and wants to protect and preserve your way of life. This is a mental change.

Ownership of your home is the evidence of choices you have made in the past about saving money. It also indicates your attitudes about money:

- 25% of home owners try to pay more than the required monthly mortgage amount

- 44% of home owners pay all their bills and are able to save money too.

4. Value

A home brings values greater than money. A secure location, resources, schools, access to hobbies, amenities, and recreation facilities are part of the decision to buy a home. The geographic area of your new home may offer much more accessibility and convenience than your previous location. This all contributes to pleasure and peace of mind.

5. Freedom to Create

By far the greatest freedom of ownership is the freedom to create the home you desire that meets your needs for expression and needs for convenience. If you want a new kitchen, go ahead and demolish the old one and create the kitchen of your dreams. If you want to knock out a wall and create one open space, it's your wall. If you want to turn the attic into a bedroom, it's your attic. If you want to paint different colors, you <u>own</u> it. If you want to add a deck for leisure or a garage workshop, you <u>own</u> it.

Many improvements that add value and convenience to your home may also add to the appraisal amount and selling price whenever you do sell. You have a feeling of greater life satisfaction, positive mindset, and greater self esteem. These are hard to measure, yet they are contagious to your family and friends. You have *ownership!*

6. Stability

Owning a home creates a feeling of belonging. Homeowners move less frequently and stay in their homes for a longer period of time than those who rent a home. When people buy a home they expect to remain there for years.

Since 2010

- 4.7% of homeowners have moved
- 26% of renters have moved

7. Stronger Ties to the Community

You choose to buy a home because you saw value and benefits in doing so. By choosing to buy a home, you are making a big step in commitment and building roots in the community. The feeling of permanency and ownership create relationships that become stable and close. When you have those close relationships you are likely to trust people to pick up your mail and feed your dogs while on vacation. This contributes to self satisfaction and peace of mind.

8. Feeling of Security

As long as you make the monthly mortgage payment you will never be evicted. Your home is your possession until you decide to sell it. Landlords make the housing decisions when you rent, can raise the rent, and can even evict you. They can choose not to renew your lease. You are not in control of the property and where you live when renting. This can feel disempowering.

9. Privacy

Privacy is priceless. Noisy next door neighbors who play loud music or have frequent fights are at some distance when you own a single family home. Choosing to own a home opens up many more choices of homes to buy. There are fewer single family homes available as rental units. Most rental units are multifamily units.

- 35% of US rental properties are single family homes
- 60% of US rentals are multi-family units

10. Control of Payments

The mortgage papers you sign contain a predictable mortgage payment for the length of the mortgage. You know what to expect. Any changes in mortgage payments will not be a surprise.

11. Children In School

Because most homeowners stay in their homes for a longer period of time, children experience a more stable home life. Children who often change schools must adjust to a new environment, new people, and new academic standards. Children of homeowners perform 9% better in math and 7% higher in reading.

12. Behavior of Children

Stability of home ownership can also affect the behavior

of children. Change in environment and separation from good friends and peers can lead to behavioral problems. Although renters can try to manage this stress, homeowners have more control of when they are moving and under what circumstances.

13. Greater Control and Peace of Mind

The sense of control that comes with home ownership produces peace of mind and contributes to better health and positive mental attitude.

- 76% of renters say that home ownership is a measure of success
- 91% of renters say that home ownership is a source of pride and accomplishment.

14. Health

Landlords don't always make it a priority to make repairs to tenant property. Mold and safety hazards slip their attention and your health may suffer. Research from the Joint Center for Housing Studies shows that home owners are healthier because they have more control over the maintenance of their home and are more likely to fix a problem caused by dampness, toxins, and allergens.

15. Pets, Pets, Pets

Every pet deserves a home. The decision to include a pet as a family member can create problems in finding rental housing that accepts pets. Home ownership keeps the family members together.

- 72% of renters have pets and they experience problems finding housing that allows pets
- 50% of pet owners are required to post a pet deposit of $200 or more
- Moving is the number one reason that families give up their pets

16. Greater Political Activity

Being more committed and tied to your community might bring opportunities to participate in local politics. Preventing crime in your neighborhood, participating in decisions regarding taxes and zoning are important to home owners. Homeowners are:

- 16% more likely to vote in local elections than renters
- More familiar with local politics and they vote to show their opinion on local matters

17. Better Quality Housing

All houses need repairs. Home owners take better care of their property because they view it as an investment. Renters often do not want to spend their money on someone else's property. Home owners who live in their house for longer periods of time care about maintenance, upkeep, and safety. Home ownership offers control over your standard of living on these items.

18. Safer Neighborhood

Active participation in a community by home owners contributes to lower crime rates. People usually watch out for each other, children, and pets. Research calculates that increasing home ownership by 1% in the US decreases the cost of violent crime by $959.8 million. Caring home owners produce a stable and safer community than areas with high turnover.

19. Better Outcomes for Children

Higher home ownership rates lead to better outcomes for children. Home ownership can affect the outcome of a child's life.

- Ownership of your home can pass on to your children
- Children of home owners earn more income
- The children are more likely to buy their own home in the future and continue the pattern of success with their family.

You may think of additional psychological values as a reason to own a home. In the next chapter we will look at financial reasons to own a home.

Price is what you pay.

VALUE IS WHAT YOU GET.

Warren Buffett

11

TEN FINANCIAL VALUES
OF HOME OWNERSHIP

There are pros and cons to everything. Home ownership brings a cash generating asset, financial benefits, and the potential accumulation of wealth. Making repairs and being responsible for the condition of the property is part of home ownership. Most people choose to buy a home because of the financial aspects. Buying a home will take one to two years to gain back the closing costs in the form of appreciation.

A person who rents a home does have some flexibility in moving as long as the lease is completed. There are no profits or tax deductions to show for renting, nothing to show but cancelled checks. Renting is appropriate for people who do not expect to remain in the same property for more than one or two years.

1. Increased Equity Produces Cash

In the time frame you own your home several financial changes are occurring.

First, the down payment you placed bought you equity in the market place. It will take about two years of appreciation to recover the costs of buying your home. This is not referring to the deposit amount, but to the costs on your settlement sheet.

Second, each monthly payment you make reduces the principal balance on a fixed loan. Your balance owed is going down.

Third, your house should be appreciating as the value goes up.

Your equity is a measure of wealth. It produces cash. You can sell your house, pay off the mortgage, and keep the remaining cash. You can sell your house and use the cash to buy another house. You have choices. The Wall Street Journal states that over the past 20 years the median value of homes has risen 81% in the US.

2. Increases Net Worth

Owning a home is the traditional method to build net worth for the average person. Add up your assets (home value, investments, savings, retirement funds, etc) and subtract your liabilities. Homes account for about 67% of the wealth of the average individual. A house is a way to store your wealth and increase net worth.

3. Appreciation Over Time

Appreciation is not an instant gain, but a longer term gain. The value of your home likely increases each year that you own it. This does depend on your geographic area. Housing market factors and economic factors greatly influence appreciation. Qualities like good schools, local employment factors, jobs from stable employers, and local resources can add value to your home. Local resources would include quality of life items (culture and education), convenience items (shopping and schools), and accessibility to them. Some houses do not always appreciate.

3.5% Annual Appreciation

The average house appreciates around 3.5% each year says Zillow economist Stan Humphries.

---

4. Less Expensive

In the long term home ownership is less expensive than renting. The more you pay up front in your down payment, the more you save in the long run. On a fixed rate mortgage, your payments will not increase as your neighborhood area improves. Renting a house in a trendy or up and coming neighborhood will bring rent increases.

5. Habits of Saving

Saving the 20% down payment requires good financial habits, discipline, and the ability to make choices toward goals. Home owners exhibit better money choices and habits.

---

38 % Less To Own

In 2016 rent costs rose by 6.5% nationally. Although more expensive to start, home ownership is 38% less costly than renting nationally. This is based o n a 30 year fixed rate mortgage with 20% down.

Trulia.com

---

6. Tax Deductions

Mortgage interest, property taxes, and some insurance premiums are tax deductible. Energy efficient additions to your home such as Energy Star appliances are also deductible. Energy Star appliances are energy efficient to lower your energy bills, and the cost of buying and installing them is a tax deduction. None of these deductions apply to renting. Capital gains exemptions may also be of benefit.

7. Second Mortgage

If you have an emergency that can be fixed with money, the equity in your home will enable you to take out a second mortgage or a home equity line of credit. You are using your home as collateral for a loan.

8. Reverse Mortgage

If needed you can draw money from your equity to create retirement income. This is like putting money into a savings account, then withdrawing it for income when you need it.

9. Rent Your Home

Many home owners go on to buy a second home. Then they rent out the first home to continue to cover the mortgage payment on that property. You now own two homes that are appreciating and increasing your net worth. The American Housing Survey states that 21.3% of home owners who have a second home do rent it out to tenants.

10. Income Property

Income property is another option of home ownership. Look at your existing home for the potential to finish the basement or any portion of the house, and create a private entrance. You can rent out this area for income and still stay in your own home. The ability to create income property is also a good criterion for buying a house.

Income Property on HGTV!

Scott McGillivray with Susan Hudson.

Watch the show **"Income Property"** with host **Scott McGillivray on HGTV** to learn about creating a rentable portion of your home. Many ideas to consider! Your renter helps pay your mortgage!

12

RENT TO OWN IS THE ANSWER

Rent to Own programs are a great solution to solve issues of credit and timing. These programs are an opportunity for you to rent a home you eventually plan to purchase. The nineteen psychological reasons and ten financial reasons to buy a home are huge. They make a difference in the quality of your life.

Everyone needs shelter. Rent To Own programs evolved as a response to changing economic conditions that have affected residential home markets. Many people have been affected by changing conditions such as job layoffs when corporations outsource functions to overseas locations, and stock market changes. Divorce, health issues, and foreclosure all have a personal impact. When new immigrants come to the US they usually have no credit history at all. All of these changing conditions created fertile ground for a change in home buying methods.

Eleven Benefits of Rent to Own

The psychological and financial benefits encourage people to buy a home. Buying a home on a Rent To Own program also has benefits of its own.

1. Option To Buy

The purchase price for Rent to Own is specified in the original agreement papers and the price is good for one year. After the first year the price will be readjusted as needed. You can often add to your agreement that additional money paid each month with the monthly rent payment can be credited toward your down payment along with your option deposit. The additional money paid goes toward your investment.

Your equity accumulates faster with this payment method than it does with a traditional mortgage payment. This is because you are not paying any interest to a lender on that additional amount you paid. Your money goes straight to the purchase price of the home and closing costs.

2. First and Last Month's Rent

Pre-paid rent for first month and last month are not part of a Rent To Own program. Your option deposit shows you are a serious home buyer. You are paying monthly rent while you work on your credit issues and intend to purchase the house. You are not a tenant intending to move to another location. So there is no pre-paid rent for first month and last month.

3. Benefit From Improvements

The more you improve the house the greater the value will be. Rent To Own programs offer a wonderful choice because you treat the house as if you already own it. You are the pre-owner.

As the "Pre-Owner" you:

- Take care of the house, yard, and repairs
- Can paint and decorate as you choose
- Can make permanent improvements

4. Time for Credit Repair

The time period for Rent To Own programs is usually one to five years. This gives time needed to establish new credit or improve credit and check for credit score improvements.

5. Fast Move In

You can find a home, post your option deposit, sign papers, and move in quickly, often in weeks. Be sure to consult with a loan officer to check your current credit in formation so you can qualify in the future to buy the home at the stated purchase price. Make sure you can afford and qualify for the payment for this home.

6. Incentives

Check with your Rent To Own company about incentives such as:

- All monthly payments made on time or early
- Credit improved by 85 points within six months.

7. Test Drive It!

You have possession of the home to live in it and have likely done a home inspection. If you decide to change your mind because of an unforeseen event, you can walk away and leave the house. You will lose your option deposit. This does not affect your credit score.

8. You Have Control

You make decisions about the house and changes you make to the property that may increase the value. You exercise control and reap the benefits.

9. Foreclosure Will Not Happen

If unforeseen events happen and you lose your job or the market changes, most owners will extend the dates of your Rent To Own program. Since you do not actually own the property yet, you will not face foreclosure.

10. Protection

You are protected in case of drastic changes in the real estate market. You do not have to continue with the agreement. You can walk away and it does not affect your credit score. Owning the house and walking away would have drastic affects on credit score if you owned the house.

11. Fixed Costs

As long as you pay the agreed upon monthly payment on time, your costs are fixed during the first year. If you go longer than one year you may have an increase in monthly rent as spelled out in your agreement papers.

12. Schools

Enroll your children in local schools. They will remain in those schools as long as you live in this home. This is your home for now and the future. You do not have to rent and then move again when you have handled your credit issues.

> **If you are not willing to learn**
> **No one can help you.**
> **If you are determined to learn**
> NO ONE CAN STOP YOU.

Six Disadvantages of Rent To Own

1. Mortgage Rates May Change

Start your Rent To Own program as soon as possible so you can work on your credit issues. Interest rates change all the time. It is possible interest rates may rise by the time you complete your home purchase. There is no way to predict this.

2. Option Deposit

Your option deposit paid up front is buying you the privilege to purchase this house, not just rent it. The option deposit is credited as your down payment at the time you qualify to purchase the house and complete closing. If you do not purchase this house, you will lose your option deposit.

3. Repairs

You are responsible for repair, maintenance, and all utilities as the "pre-owner." The more care you give your house the more it can appreciate. You will enjoy all the financial benefits when you actually purchase the house.

4. Late Payments

Making any late monthly payments will void your Rent To Own agreement. You need to be completely committed to the program to accomplish your goal of home ownership.

5. Mortgage Qualifying

You need to work hard to improve your credit score and establish a credit file that a lender will accept. Only you can do this for yourself. There is no guarantee you will be approved for a mortgage loan in the time frame you agreed upon for this house.

6. Paper Trail of Records

Qualifying for a mortgage loan requires that you must meet the criteria of the bank. You will need to submit all the right records with the right amounts on them. This includes W2 statements from a job or two years of tax returns from a business you started. Your credit records and credit score must meet requirements. Your income must qualify for the purchase price of the home. The whole picture must be consistent.

Who Is A Good Match For Rent To Own?

• Someone who has cash to put down now and

• Needs time to work on their credit issues to improve their credit score or create a credit file and get approval for a bank mortgage loan

8 Steps For Rent to Own

1. Cash Deposit

You will need 10% to 20% to put down as an option deposit. This becomes your down payment when you actu-ally buy the house.

2. Credit Score

Check your credit score to see what accounts need attention to raise your score. This may require months or years before you can actually own the home.

3. Join Our Buyer's List

Go to our website and join our Buyer's List to get immediate e-mail announcements of recent additions to our Rent To Own program.

4. Choose A Home

Find a house you like that is available on a Rent To Own program.

5. Application

Complete the Rent To Own or Work To Own application and submit it with your option deposit check.

- This money is your "option deposit."
- It guarantees your "option" to buy the house.
- No one else can buy the house as long as you make your rent payments on time.
- Your deposit is not refundable.

- Employment will be verified.
- Salary will be verified.

6. Sign the Papers

Papers will show the number of years you will pay rent while you work to improve your credit score. Usually this is one to five years. When your credit score is good enough, you will apply to a bank to get a loan to own your home.

7. Closing With An Attorney.

Your option deposit becomes your down payment at the time of purchase. At closing, you sign the papers and the mortgage is in your name.

8. Find A Work To Own Home

A home that needs work is called a "fixer-upper" or a "handy-man special." Programs for Work To Own homes exist for people who have skills, experience, and resources to make improvements to a home they choose. This is likely someone in the construction business or who has access to construc-tion resources. A list is made of agreed upon improvements with a schedule for the work to be inspected. This completed work adds to the value of the home.

Often you can get these houses at a good price if you are will-ing and have skills and experience to make the repairs yourself. Do not take on repairs if you do not have the experience.

Rent To Own and **Work To Own** programs are a tool to help people get into their very own home. Let us know how we can help you!

Fixer Upper on HGTV

Check the TV listings for HGTV and watch the show "Fixer Upper" with hosts Chip and Joanna Gaines. Many ideas to consider! You can Work To Own a fixer upper and use your money and time to make renova-tions agreed upon while you live there. Your work and time add to the appraisal value of the house. This type of house is often called a "handyman special."

CountryLiving.com

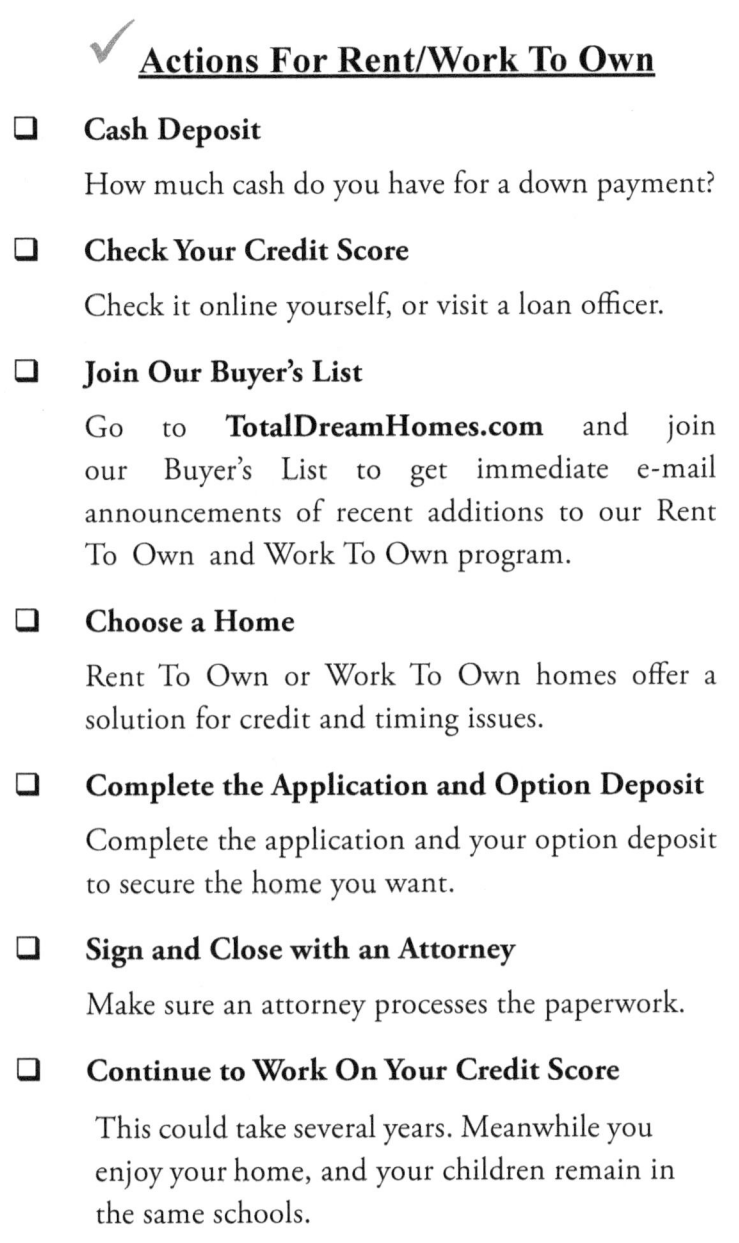

✓ **<u>Actions For Rent/Work To Own</u>**

❑ **Cash Deposit**

How much cash do you have for a down payment?

❑ **Check Your Credit Score**

Check it online yourself, or visit a loan officer.

❑ **Join Our Buyer's List**

Go to **TotalDreamHomes.com** and join our Buyer's List to get immediate e-mail announcements of recent additions to our Rent To Own and Work To Own program.

❑ **Choose a Home**

Rent To Own or Work To Own homes offer a solution for credit and timing issues.

❑ **Complete the Application and Option Deposit**

Complete the application and your option deposit to secure the home you want.

❑ **Sign and Close with an Attorney**

Make sure an attorney processes the paperwork.

❑ **Continue to Work On Your Credit Score**

This could take several years. Meanwhile you enjoy your home, and your children remain in the same schools.

✓ Take Action!

If you are interested in checking out Rent To Own and Work To Own programs and how our programs can meet your needs, please call:

24 Hour Buyer Information: (703) 232-1750

24 Hour Seller Information: (703) 232-1600

And

Join Our Buyer's List

If you are serious about finding a home on a Rent To Own or Work To Own program, go to our website:

TotalDreamHomes.com

You will be on the list to receive immediate e-mails for houses added to our program. $99 set up fee.

www.ingramcontent.com/pod-product-compliance
Lightning Source LLC
Chambersburg PA
CBHW070045210526
45170CB00012B/585